D1611246

PRACTICAL AUTO DETAILING AT HOME

Rourke M. O'Brien & John B. Thomas

Copyright © 1992
Beeman Jorgensen, Inc.

ISBN 0-929758-05-6

All rights reserved including
the right of reproduction in whole
or in any part without permission
from the publisher.

Published by Beeman Jorgensen, Inc.
7510 Allisonville Road, Suite 117, Indianapolis, IN 46250 U.S.A.

Printed and bound in the United States of America
Cover design by Flack Design, Indianapolis, Indiana

First Printing, August 1992

Contents

WHAT YOU'LL NEED

"A driveway, a hose and elbow grease"

For the average car owner, the requirements for washing a car form a pretty short list: a hose, a bucket, a sponge and some dish soap. For the owner of a show car, the list could be as long as this entire book—these people often have special crates just for their cleaning supplies.

What we suggest here is something in between those two extremes. Our list of items includes everything you'll need to make your car look great, but it does not include so much that you'll go broke or have to add on to your garage.

Three of the ingredients are obvious: you need a water source, a driveway or other clean work area and you need a few hours you can spending working on your car.

We've included a handful of items that are optional, and in some instances we have suggested specific brands that we think are especially good. For the most part, we have listed the items in the order in which they appear in the text.

If at all possible, we suggest that you have all of the items on our list on hand before you start on your car to make sure you don't get halfway through a step and then find out you don't have what you need to finish. All of the items on our list can be bought at your nearest auto parts or discount store. Prices and availability of some items may vary, but, by shopping around a little bit, you should be able to find everything you

need at a reasonable price. One basic rule of thumb is to keep the tools simple, but be sure you have good tools. For example, a good, metal hose nozzle may cost a little more than a plastic one, but it will last longer and perform better.

Although at the end of this chapter we have a complete list of the items you'll need, some of which are pretty self-explanatory: a garden hose with a nozzle, a two-gallon bucket and a wash mitt, preferably lamb's wool, this chapter will focus on those items which may require furhter explanation.

For soap, we cannot recommend strongly enough that you not use any kind of dish soap—they are much too harsh for use on your car and do not rinse away as easily as is necessary. Instead, we recommend a low-PH soap made

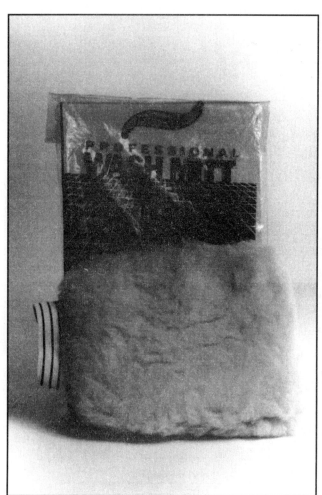

Car wash soaps are available from most car-care companies.

For best results, a lamb's wool mitt should be used.

specifically for washing cars. Most of the major car-care companies make a soap.

You should also be sure to have on hand plenty of clean towels. We have found that soft terry cloth is best. We recommend that certain towels be used for particular jobs every time you clean your car. For example, have one or two towels that are used for cleaning the engine, and a few that are used only for removing wax. If the towels are all the same color and size, mark them with indelible marker to keep them separated (you could put a "W" on the ones used for washing, a "D" on the ones used for drying, an "X" on the ones used for waxing, etc..). That way, you won't run the risk of mixing them up and rubbing engine gunk into your paint. We recommend using towels to dry your car rather than chamois, simply because we have found them to do a better job. The towels should be machine washed and dried between every use. Keep them separated according to use even when washing them—for example, don't wash engine towels in the same load as the drying towels.

You'll find that we recommend using a number of different types of brushes for cleaning your car. While you can buy "detail brushes" at most auto parts stores, many household brushes will do the same job for less money. The basic brushes you will need are: a soft-bristle tooth brush; a stiff-bristle tooth brush; a hand brush for tires; another hand brush for cleaning carpets and floor mats; and a soft-bristle brush (like the ones used for basting in the kitchen) which will be used to remove dust from different parts of the interior. Use each brush for a particular task, marking each one according to what it is used for.

You'll also need an all-purpose cleaner. Many companies make these and they are formulated to break up grease and tough stains. We have found Simple Green to be the best all-purpose cleaner, but many others do a good job. The bug sponge we recommend is a 5-1/4" x 4" "professional" bug sponge distributed by SM Arnold Inc. Both Simple Green and the bug sponges can be bought at any auto parts store.

Although other companies make all-purpose cleaners, we have found Simple Green to be the best.

Professional bug sponges will remove bugs and grit without scratching your car.

Some items you may not have expected to be included in this book are steel wool, masking tape, cotton swabs and toothpicks. For steel wool, get #0000 grade, It's soft enough that it won't hurt your car's surface, yet strong enough to get the job done. The masking tape will be used to remove lint from convertible tops and interior cloth and carpets. The cotton swabs and toothpicks will be used for some of the final touches that make detailing what it is.

Below is a complete list of what you'll need to perform your driveway detail:

1. Hose
2. Nozzle
3. Two-gallon bucket
4. Lamb's wool wash mitt
5. Clean terry-cloth towels
6. A low-PH car-wash soap
7. Wheel and tire cleaner
8. Stiff and soft-bristle tooth brushes
9. Two tire brushes (or hand brushes) one for tires, one for the interior
10. All-purpose cleaner
11. A plastic bag or plastic wrap (optional)
12. Engine degreaser (optional)
13. Silicone-based rubber and vinyl protectant
14. #0000-grade steel wool
15. Electric hair dryer (optional)
16. High-heat paint (optional)
17. Wide masking tape
18. Bug sponge
19. Plastic-window polish (optional)
20. Polishing compound
21. Rubbing compound (optional)
22. Two wax applicator pads
23. Vinyl dressing (optional)

Many companies offer wheel and tire cleaners.

Vinyl and rubber protectants add gloss to vinyl and rubber surfaces.

Polishing compounds will remove old wax and oxidized paint.

Rubbing compounds are for especially tough paint problems

High-heat paints will last longer on hot surfaces.

Some manufacturers offer special polishes for mag wheels.

THE ENGINE COMPARTMENT, WHEELS AND DOOR JAMBS

"Clean, shiny and black"

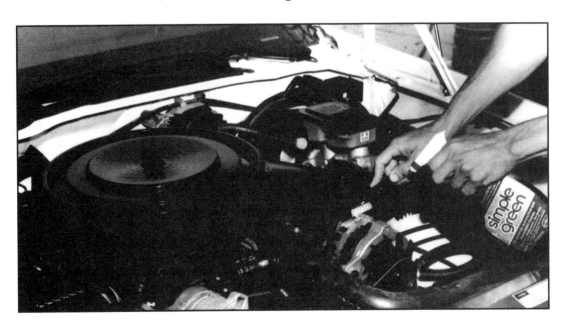

It will surprise some people to learn that the first step in automotive detailing is cleaning the engine, wheels and door jambs. Most of us have for years begun cleaning the car by hosing down and washing the outside of the car, working our way around the body and ending with the interior and windows. Then we *might* do the wheels, but usually even a thorough cleaning didn't include so much as opening the hood, let alone scrubbing the engine, engine compartment and door jambs.

But, detailing starts on these less-exciting parts for a couple of reasons. First of all, it makes sense to clean the grimiest part of the car first so you don't later slop engine or wheel dirt onto clean paint. Secondly, doing these parts first lets you get some of the most detail-oriented work out of the way first.

Please note that, while cleaning these grimier parts of the car, we will be recommending that you use some solvents or degreasers. These chemicals should be used carefully, and label directions should be read and followed closely.

To begin, use your hose to spray the entire car with water, rinsing away as much of the dust and dirt as will come off easily. Then attack the wheels, spraying them one at a time with a wheel and tire cleaner and scrubbing them with a stiff-bristle toothbrush. Work in and around spokes or other wheel decorations, brushing away road grime and brake dust. Do not allow the cleaner to sit on a wheel too long, because it might actually damage some softer metals. Do one wheel at a time, and rinse each one

Begin your job by spraying the entire car with water.

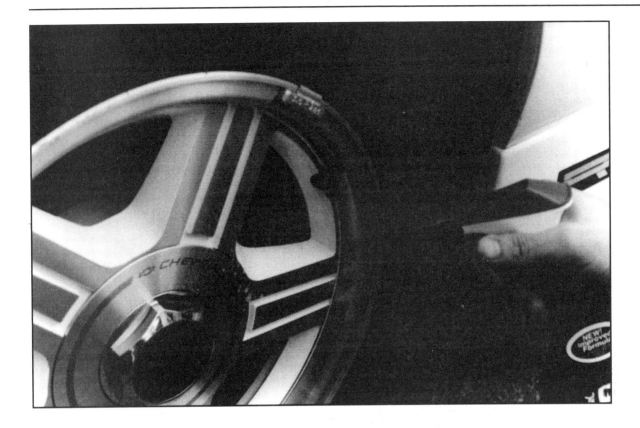

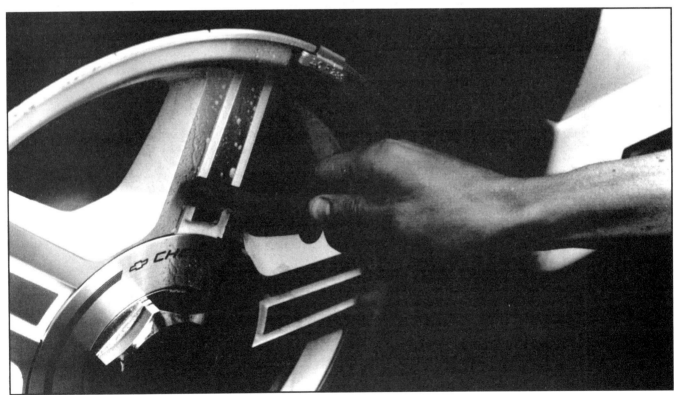

Spray the all-purpose cleaner onto the wheels and then scrub with a toothbrush.

completely before moving to the next. Also, as you are working, do not get the cleaner on the painted parts of the car. It won't hurt the paint immediately, but it could do serious damage to your car's surface if it's not rinsed off quickly. Because some wheels are made of soft alloys, do not use abrasive cleaners or scouring pads to clean them. Simply work with the cleaner and a brush until the wheel is cleaned. For wheels that are not very dirty, the cleaner may be able to do almost all of the work, requiring just a little bit of brushing to break up hardened dirt.

As you wash the wheels, you might also want to wash the tires, using a tire cleaner to break up dirt, but this time using a tire brush (commonly known as a hand brush). Again, do not let the cleaner sit on the rubber too long, but rinse it off quickly. You may also want to follow by washing the tires again with a hand brush and soapy water. As you rinse the wheels and tires for the last time, spray up under the wheel wells to break up any dirt that may have collected there.

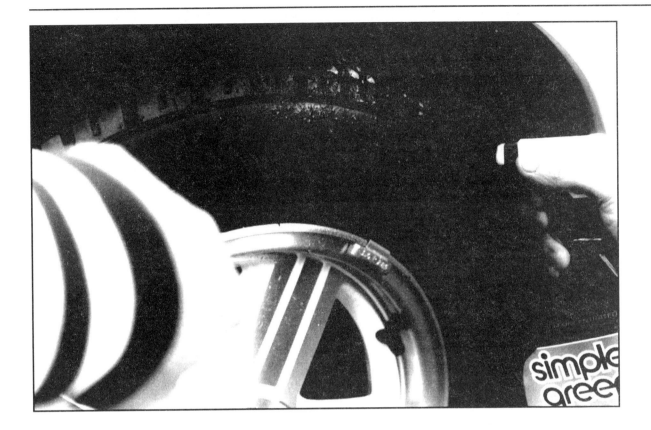

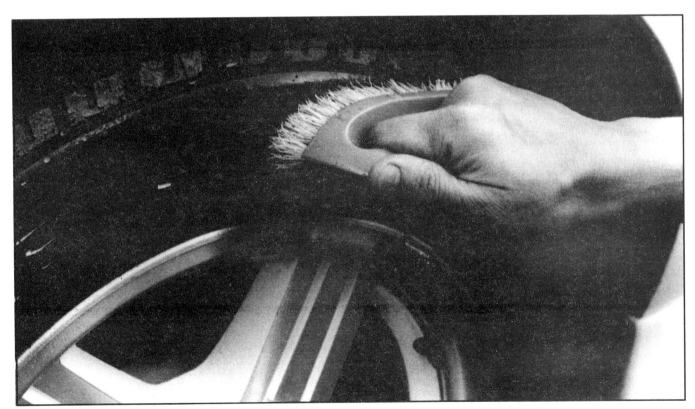

Clean the tires with the all-purpose cleaner and a hand brush.

After scrubbing and rinsing all four wheels and tires, rinse the area under and around the car so you don't later splash the grime onto your car.

Next you'll want to open each door to clean the door jambs and edges of the doors. This should be done for two reasons: because dirty doors and jambs can make even the cleanest car look bad; and, because it helps prevent the rust that sometimes begins in out-of-the-way places.

So, using soapy water, a wash mitt and a brush, wash the door edges and jambs thoroughly. For more difficult grime, you may want to use the all-purpose cleaner, but rinse it off quickly. A toothbrush will be helpful in getting dirt out of the ridges in the running boards and door vents and from around the doors' working parts. While you're cleaning the jambs, open the doors to different positions to make sure you are

getting the dirt from all the nooks and crannies. The rubber pieces around the doors collect a lot of dirt and dust, so spread them open and use the brush to clean them out. Clean the painted areas in the door jambs every bit as well as you will the exterior, because later you will wax them. Rinse the door jambs by letting water flow softly over them or by wiping them down with a wet sponge or mitt. Don't worry about drying them now. We'll do that later.

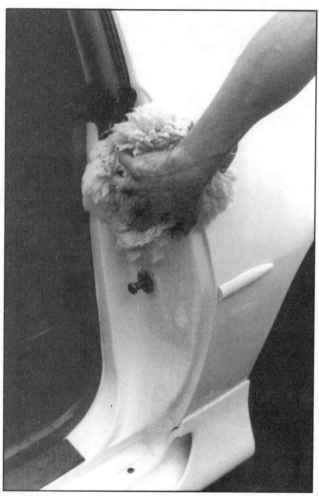

Clean the door jambs with sudsy water.

Rinse the wheels and tires with a strong stream of water.

Use a brush to get grit out of the running boards.

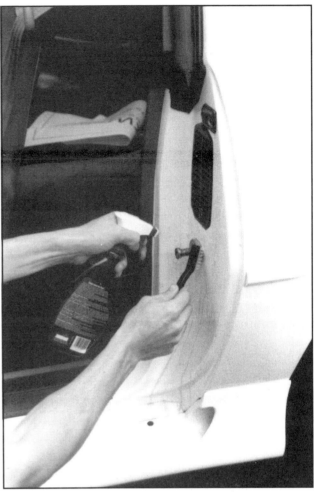

Difficult grime will require attention with the all-purpose cleaner and a brush.

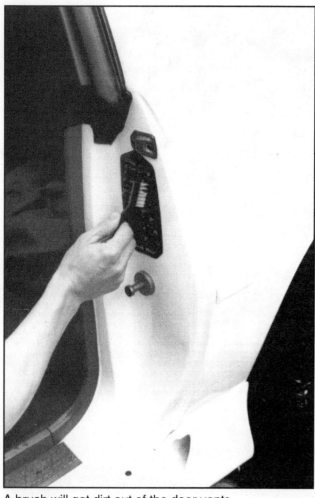

A brush will get dirt out of the door vents.

Spray the door jambs, taking care not to soak the carpet in the interior.

Next, open the trunk. While we won't recommend cleaning the interior of the trunk now, we do suggest that you clean the painted parts inside the trunk now. Use the same procedures you used for cleaning the inside of the door jambs, washing the painted areas with soapy water and using the all-purpose cleaner on especially dirty areas. Obviously, you need to be careful about getting inside of the trunk too wet, so rinse the areas with a damp towel or by running water gently over them. Pay special attention to rinsing out the gutters around the trunk, since these areas often are allowed to get very dirty, giving rust a good place to start. Get these areas as clean as you would any other painted parts because you will wax these areas just as you will the painted areas in the door jambs.

Now we turn to the engine compartment. This is one area where many auto enthusiasts spend a great deal of time, breaking the engine down and cleaning or even painting individual pieces. In the interest of keeping things simple, though, the most engine tinkering we will suggest is that you may want to cover your distributor cap with a plastic bag or plastic wrap before spraying water onto your engine.

However, before doing any cleaning under your car's hood, be sure the engine has cooled enough that you won't be burned, but not so much that the grease has hardened. Rinse the engine with a gentle spray. A lot of dirt and dust will wash away with the rinse, but stubborn grime and grease will require a more direct effect.

A plastic bag will help to keep the distributor cap dry.

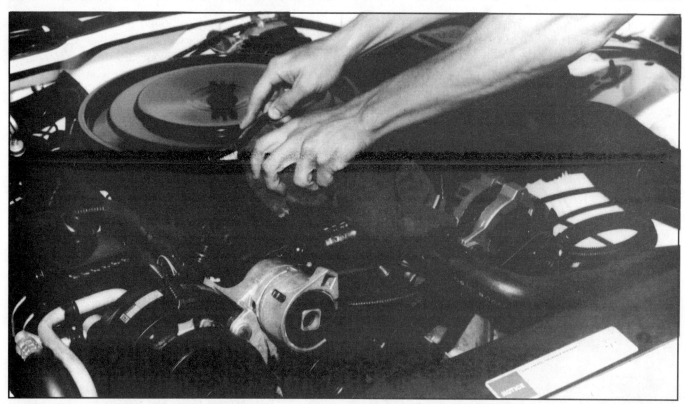

A brush will help cut through engine grime.

Rinse the engine with a gentle spray.

Using the all-purpose cleaner, scrub away grime and oil. Either spray the cleaner onto a brush or apply it directly onto the engine, using the brush and a stiff scrubbing motion to cut through the grease. Work on one section at a time, applying the cleaner and then rinsing it before moving on to the next section. Use a nozzle on the hose to get a high-pressure water stream. Remember: If the cleaner is allowed to sit on the engine too long, it may dry and become difficult to remove.

The cleaner will do most of the work, but a toothbrush may be required to get to some of the tighter areas. A few of the spots may require more than one pass, but others will come clean pretty easily. Use towels or brushes as needed, finding out what works best for you. Don't be afraid to reach under and around hoses and engine parts, and certainly don't shy away from getting your hands dirty.

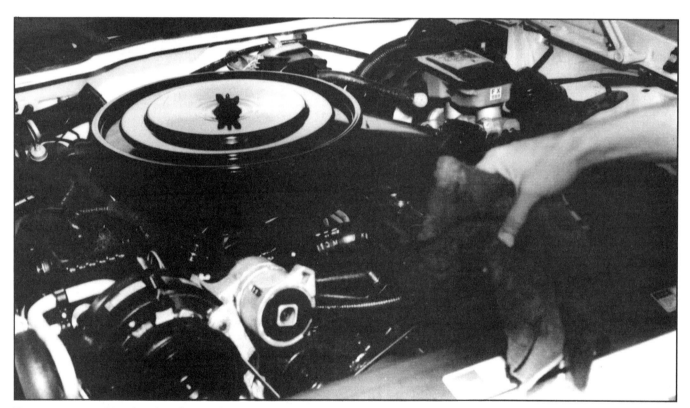

Towels work well in cleaning the engine.

For especially tough grime, an engine degreaser may be required, but take special care when using degreasers and follow label directions carefully. Throughout this process, it is important to keep your tools clean, so rinse the brushes and towels often. Also rinse the soap and old dirt away from engine surfaces so you can keep track of what you have and haven't done and so you can see how well you're doing. Let the chemicals do as much of the work as possible, but do not think that allowing them to sit longer on the engine will improve their effectiveness. It will simply damage engine parts. Continually rinse what you have cleaned.

Gunk is a popular engine degreaser.

Apply the degreaser to especially grimy areas.

Clean your tools often.

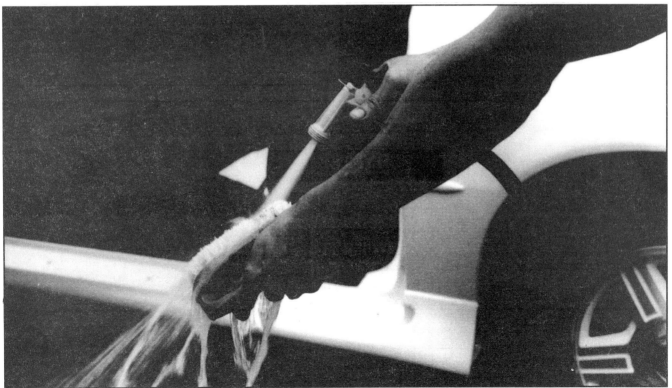

Next, work on the engine compartment, cleaning any painted surfaces as you would if they were on the outside of the car. This work will be similar to the work you did on the door jambs. The all-purpose cleaner will work well, and a toothbrush will be helpful to get into the tricky areas. Be especially sure to clean out the drainage trough that runs along the back and sides of the engine compartment. Wash the underside of the hood, using a brush and the all-purpose cleaner to break up any gunk that may found its way there. Follow up with a soapy wash, and then rinse thoroughly.

After giving the whole engine and engine compartment one final rinse, spray the driveway under the car, washing away all grit and dirt and any cleaners on the ground. Clean your tools and cleaner containers before putting them away. Rinse the bucket.

Next, dry the engine and engine compartment, using towels that will not be used for anything else. Although you have cleaned the engine, leftover cleaner or engine grime could be picked up by the towels. If you were to then use these same towels on the exterior or windows, you could do some serious damage. Have one or two towels that you always use for the engine and engine compartment, and never use them for anything else.

When drying around the engine, remember that the engine compartment—surfaces painted with the same paint as the exterior—will be waxed with the rest of the car, so they must be as clean as you want the whole car to be.

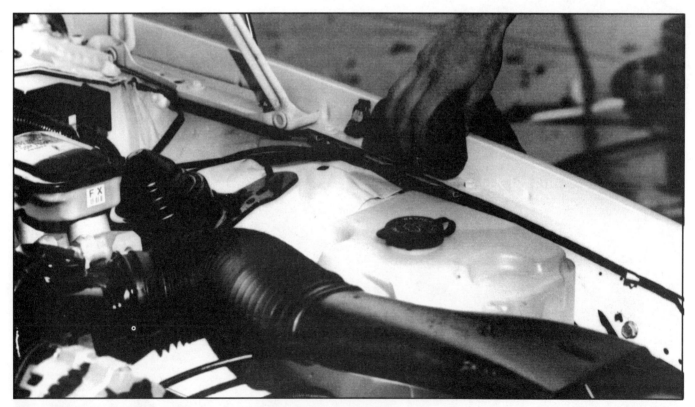

Pay special attention to the gutters around the engine compartment.

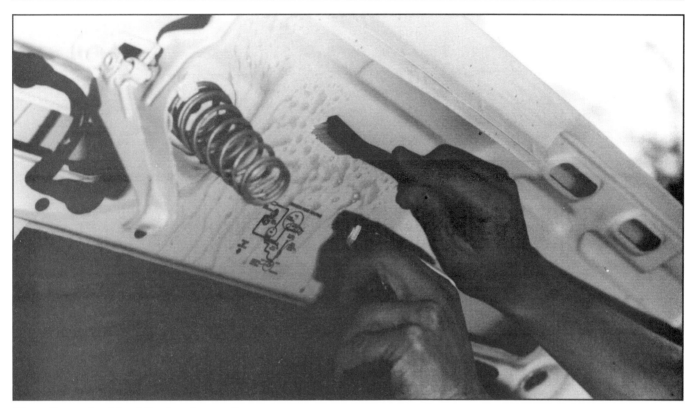

Clean the underside of the hood as well.

Dry the engine and engine compartment so you can apply a rubber and vinyl protectant.

Once the engine is dry, spray a silicone-based rubber and vinyl protectant onto all black surfaces, including the battery case, hoses, wire casings and rubber or plastic covers. Apply the silicone generously, but be sure to spray it evenly to cover all of the surfaces you are spraying. Nothing looks worse than a shiny black hose that has a grey-brown underside because it was missed. As you apply the spray, avoid getting it onto chrome or painted areas because it can be difficult remove from those surfaces and could leave a haze or film if not cleaned off completely.

Once you have sprayed the silicone on all black surfaces, close the hood and continue working on the rest of the car. Removing the silicone will be one of the last things we do, because the longer it can sit and work into the rubber, the better. Remember, the silicone is used not only to make the black surfaces look good, but also to protect and preserve them. Therefore, the longer it sits, the better is is for your car. Letting it sit for as long as three or four hours will not harm any of the engine parts.

When the time comes to remove the silicone, use a towel, wiping away every part that was sprayed and, again, being sure the coverage was even and complete. This is also a good time to wipe the rest of the engine and compartment dry, but be careful not to wipe the silicone off of one part and then, by using that same towel, wiping it onto chrome or paint. Again, do not use the towel from this job on any other part of the car, because it will cloud a chrome or painted finish. Also, be sure to remove as much of the excess silicone as possible, because some water-based silicone products may, over time, take on a whitish sheen that takes away from the shine.

To remove rust or stubborn water spots from chrome, use #0000 grade steel wool after the surface has dried, scrubbing lightly and wiping away any dust or residue with a towel.

Apply the protectant to all black surfaces.

Remove the silicone treatment with a towel after finishing the rest of the car.

Use grade #0000 steel wool.

If you did not cover your distributor cap and you are afraid you may have gotten water under it, you will want to remove the cap and dry the inside of it with an electric hair dryer.

Although you will eventually wax the painted areas under the hood, you should wait until you wax the rest of the car. If you want to paint some of the engine parts, now is the time to do it. While we do not necssarily recommend trying to paint individual engine parts to match their original colors, we do understand that rusty-looking parts can detract from the look of an engine. Even so, we suggest that you be extremely careful when using paint on your engine, and we have found that it usually is not necessary.

If you do decide that you want to paint, though, use a high-heat paint and mask off areas you do not want painted. Read and follow label directions closely. Prepare the areas to be painted by scrubbing them with steel wool, roughing up the surfaces so they will hold the paint better. Apply the paint in short, quick burst so you can keep track of what you are painting and how well the paint is going on. Shake the can often, applying the pain evenly to get the minimum effective coverage. Putting too much paint on these surface will take away from the painted look, and a gloppy, heavy paint job will look worse than no paint job at all.

After you have finished cleaning, siliconing, and polishing your engine compartment, take a step back and look at it. Although you still haven't waxed painted areas, what you'll see probably looks better than it has since the car was brand new.

If water did get under the distributor cap, it may be dried with a hair dryer.

THE EXTERIOR

"Clean, smooth and polished"

So, the wheels and tires are clean and everything under the hood is looking good. Now we come to the part of the car that most people consider to be the only part that needs regular cleaning: the exterior. It can be the easiest part of the car to clean—you simply wipe it down with soapy water and hose it off. Presto—you've got a clean car. But to do it right, to detail your car, requires a lot more.

Almost everybody has a different feeling about how to wash a car's exterior. Some people wash a car by leaving it out in the rain. Others clean their cars

with cotton swabs and a tooth brush. In between those extremes are hundreds of things for people to disagree on, but one of the most basic points of disagreement is soap.

For years, a lot of people have used dish soap on their cars, whipping it up with lots of bubbles and giving the car a brisk scrub. Now, nearly everyone agrees that nothing could be worse for a car's paint than detergent soaps. In fact, many

believe that a car with a good coat of wax should be washed only with water and a mitt. For this chapter, though, we're going to assume your car needs a thorough cleaning.

To begin, spray the car with water. There's no reason to use a lot of water pressure, since you're just trying to wet the car, not clean it off. In fact, you really don't need the spray nozzle on the hose.

Begin the exterior cleaning by hosing down the entire car again.

Next, attack any bugs and tar on the car with the all-purpose cleaner and what is known as a professional bug sponge. You'll want to clean one section at a time, spraying the cleaner onto parts of the car facing the front and onto the sides of the car from the middle on down. Use the bug sponge to wipe the bugs and tar off of the car, rinsing immediately. Work in one area at a time so the cleaner sits on the car long enough to work but not long enough to damage the car's paint. About two minutes is the most time a cleaner should be on your car.

Start with the front of the car, including the headlights, grill, and spoiler, and work around to the sides. Be sure to include the fronts of the side mirrors and the windshield in this process. Also work on the frame around the windshield, the windshield wipers and blades, and any spoilers or flares that could catch bugs. Pay special attention to the areas just behind the wheels, because this is where the majority of the tar and road film will build up. Again, work on the sides of the car quickly, getting the cleaner off of the paint as quickly as possible. As you work your way to the back of the car, use

a cleaner and bug sponge on the tip of the exhaust pipe to help remove any carbon build-up. Rinse the bug sponge often, and rinse the car as you go along. Then take a second pass, checking to make sure all the bugs and tar have been removed. Should you find missed spots, spray the cleaner onto the pad this time, wipe the spot away and rinse. Again, be sure to clean the sponge often. If a small rock or hard piece of dirt should get stuck in the sponge, it could scratch your paint.

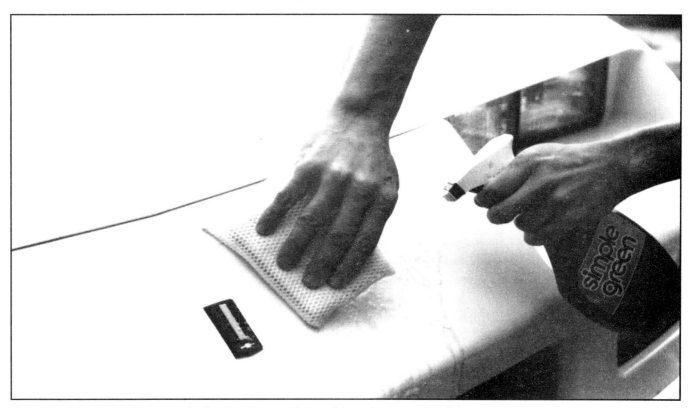

Use the all-purpose cleaner and a bug sponge to clean all front-facing parts of the car.

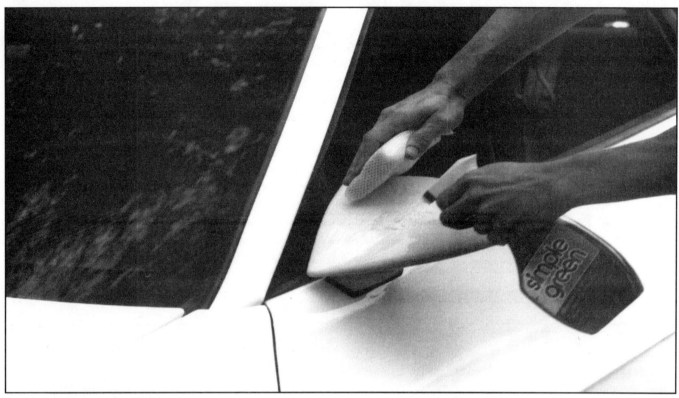
Include the side mirrors in the initial cleaning process.

Be sure to clean the area above the windshield.

Rinse the car thoroughly after these steps, and be sure to rinse the ground around the car as well, so you won't be stepping in washed-off solvents, dragging the hose across them or splashing them onto the car.

If your car has a vinyl or convertible top, you'll want to clean the top with the all-purpose cleaner and a hand brush. Spray the cleaner onto the surface and scrub briskly with the brush, paying special attention to cleaning the front of the top and the edges. If the car has any vinyl moldings or accents, you'll want to do them now as well, using the same cleaner and brush. Be sure to work quickly with the cleaner, rinsing the top and other areas often as you work, and rinse thoroughly after you've finished to make sure the cleaner hasn't puddled anywhere on the top.

For cars with cloth tops, wash the top with a mild (low PH) soap and a brush. To remove lint from the top, wrap a piece of masking tape around your hand with the sticky side out and dab at the top to lift away lint.

If the car has a plastic back window, you should be careful cleaning because the plastic is generally very soft. Wash the window with a mild soap and a mitt, taking care not to scratch the window. To help maintain the window, you may want to apply a plastic window polish, which should be available at an auto parts store.

Next, using your car soap and a lamb's wool mitt, wash the car, going over the spots you have already cleaned, including the tires and wheels, once again. If you are working in bright sunlight or very high heat, be careful not to let the soap dry on the car. Work on small sections only. There is no reason to apply a lot of pressure—the dirt should come off without too much work—since pressing too hard will scratch the paint.

Tar and Bug Remover may be necessary behind the wheel wells.

If the car is especially dirty, empty your bucket and refill it with a fresh soap mixture and clean your mitt often. Once the whole car has been washed, go around the car with your soft-bristle toothbrush and soapy water, working to get old wax out of tight areas. Wax often builds up around emblems, in nooks and crannies, around door handles and seals and around headlights. To clean these spots, brush soapy water onto the spot and allow the water to soften the wax. Then go back over the spots again with the brush to remove the wax. Work around the edges of the trunk lid, the grille and hood, paying special attention to emblems that have raised letters. Again, rinse each

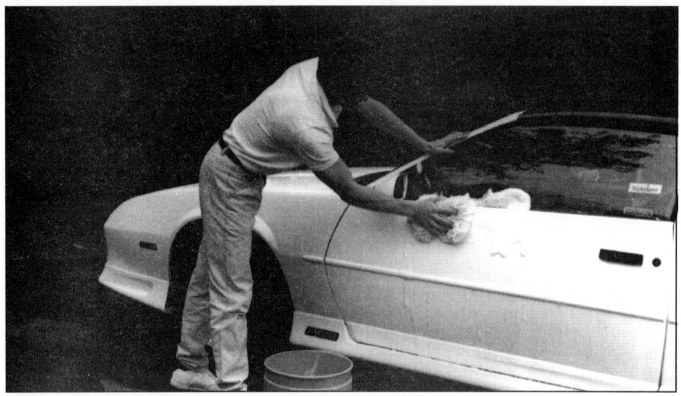

Wash the exterior with a sudsy mixture and a lamb's wool mitt.

area as you work on it so the soap is not allowed to dry on the car.

After you have completely washed the car, rinse it one final time without a nozzle on the hose. Be sure to flush out the areas around bumpers and other places where soapy water could have collected.

Next, thoroughly dry the car, including windows, door jambs and under the hood and trunk lid. It is important that the car be entirely dry before you go on to the next step. Once you begin using polishes, running into even a drop of water will take away from the shiny finish you're looking for., So, again, make sure the car is completely dry before proceeding.

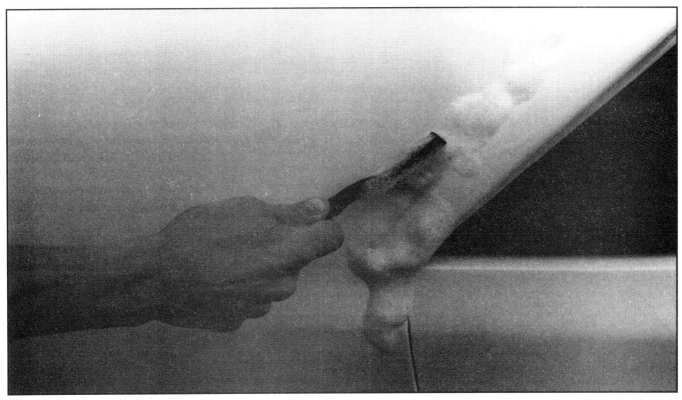

Use a toothbrush to remove old wax.

Opposite Page: Simple masking tape will help remove lint from cloth tops. Use only plastic polishes on plastic back windows.

Rinse the car without a nozzle on the hose.

Thoroughly dry the car with clean towels.

At this point, we need to talk about paint. Car makers use a variety of different paint processes. Some companies apply countless coats of paint to build up a deep finish. Others paint the car and then apply a clear coat that seals the paint onto your car, almost like plastic coating. As different as these processes may sound, they can be treated pretty much the same when it comes to cleaning. So, regardless of what kind of paint your car has, we're going to take you through some stages that will help you clean it, leaving a smooth, clean and easy-to-wax surface.

What we need to do is use a polishing compound to take away surface scratches and remove dirt and oxidation from the surface of the paint. What is oxidation? Basically, it is dead paint. The paints used on cars have oils in them, and when that oil dries out, you are left with a chalky dust. When you use a polishing compound on the car, you are taking away the dead paint that has lost its oils. When you follow up with wax that contains a conditioner, you are then replacing oils that were removed in the polishing process, reviving the "new" paint you have exposed.

Before we start, we want to warn you that polishing compounds are abrasive and can damage your car's paint if you are not careful. Nonetheless, some cars may require even more drastic measures: a rubbing compound, which is even more harsh than the polishing compound. However, we have found that a polishing compound usually will do the job.

Because this process involves removing surface scratches, dirt and "dead" paint, we must also warn you that the cloth you use to remove the polishing compound may be slightly colored by the paint. Depending on the color of your car, the paint will come off in different amounts—car with a clear-coat finish probably will have almost no paint rubbing off on to the rag, while

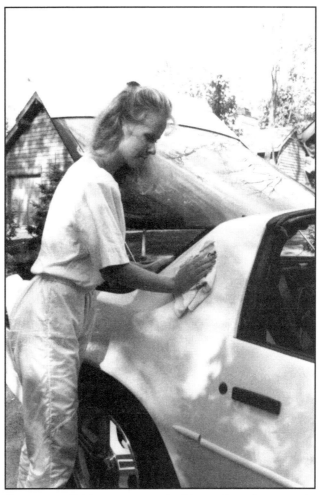

Remove polishing compound with another clean towel, turning the towel frequently.

cars with red paint will leave the most color on the cloth. Do not panic if this happens. It is a sign that you are removing the "dead" paint. The objective is to get a smooth finish that will take wax easily. Although applying and removing a polishing compound will take some work, once you have completed this part, the wax will go on and off easily.

Cars with serious damage to the paint may require a rubbing compound instead of a polishing compound. Be warned, however, that rubbing compounds can do damage to the car's finish if they are used incorrectly. Rubbing compounds are only for the most serious of conditions, and should be used only as a last resort. Because they have such an effect on a car's finish, it is difficult to use them on some spots and not others, so we suggest avoiding them altogether if possible.

To get an idea of how much of a difference a polishing compound can make, use it on a small part of your car. Apply and remove it according to the directions on the can, and then rub the cleaned area with the back of your hand. Now rub your hand on another part of the car. You'll feel the difference immediately. The part you have cleaned with the polishing compound will be smooth and grit-free. The other part will be rough and, although you have washed the car, will feel gritty.

Another way to see the difference is by looking at how much dirt remains in the paint after washing and how clean an area looks after it has been cleaned with a polishing compound. Dirt actually gets into the paint on your car, and simple washing cannot remove it all. But, polishing compound can because it removes the old paint, taking dirt and surface scratches with it. While you will see that the polishing compound pulls out many of the small scratches in the paint, don't try to use the compound to remove deep scratches or all scratches—you could do a lot of damage trying to make the compound do too much.

Applying and removing the compound is simple, and the directions on the can should be self-explanatory. Be sure to use a damp applicator pad (not the same one you will use for the wax) and work in circles that overlap each other, making sure to completely cover the paint. Keep an even amount of pressure on the the pad in applying and removing the compound so that the result is a smooth-looking finish. Rubbing too hard will remove too much paint, hurting the look of your car. It is important to use the polishing compound on all exposed areas of your car, although there is no reason to use this process on the painted areas in the door jambs or under your hood or in the trunk. Weather is the biggest reason your paint loses its clean shine. Bright sunshine bakes the shine out and rain and wind put dirt on your car. Therefore, it's not necessary to try to deep clean those places that aren't exposed to the weather.

Remove the compound with a dry, clean cloth (again, not the same one you will use for removing wax), turning the cloth often. Be careful to remove all of the compound.

After you have used the polishing compound on your entire car, begin the waxing process right away. You don't want your car to sit without a protective coat of wax on it. The sun will quickly bake your paint, doing more damage than if you had left the layer of dirty paint on your car.

As we said before, since you have rubbed all the dirt and roughness off of your car's paint, waxing will be much easier than you are probably used to. Most people think of waxing as the most difficult part of cleaning a car, but most people wax their cars without removing all the dirt from the paint. With its smooth finish, your car will be a breeze to wax.

The wax you will want to use on your car is a natural wax with as few cleaning additives as possible., A wax like this will be easy to apply, will replenish oils the paint has lost and will leave you with a clean, polished finish.

When applying the wax, remember that more is not necessarily better. Because you have already cleaned the paint thoroughly, you do not need to try to use the wax to clean it further. Simply be sure you get complete coverage with the wax and apply it with an even coating.

Using a wax applicator, apply the wax to the outside of the car first, doing door jambs and the areas under the hood and in the trunk later. Apply it in over-

Wax your car using a natural wax with few cleaning additives.

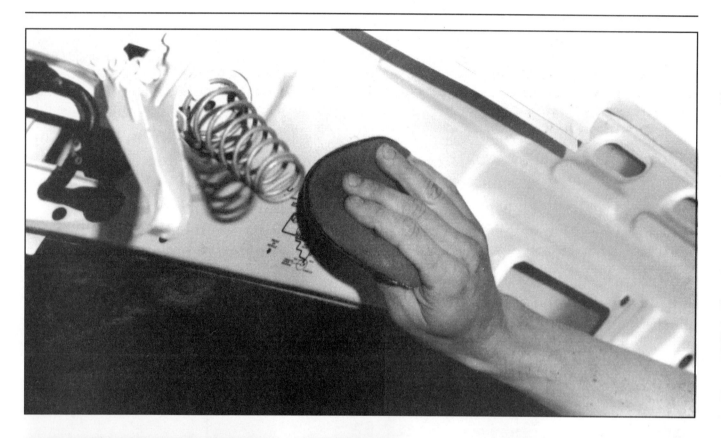

Wax areas under the hood and in the trunk and doorjambs.

lapping circles, being sure not to miss any spots.

The weather will determine how much of the car you should do at a time. If the sun is bright and hot, you will want to apply the wax to a small area at a time, wiping the wax off between applications. However, on a cloudy and cool day, you will be able to wax larger areas of the car at a time. Remember, the objective is not to let the wax bake onto the car's finish but just to let it dry. Use your common sense. If the wax is terribly difficult to remove, chances are you waited too long. However, if it is still wet, you are removing it too soon. To remove the wax, we recommend using a soft, terry cloth towel. Other cloths—such as cheese cloth—are popular for removing wax, but we have found the good, old-fashioned towels work best for us.

If your car has a removable hard top, clean and wax it with the rest of the car and then carefully remove it. Now clean and wax the painted parts that were under the top, paying special attention to the places where the top actually sits on the car.

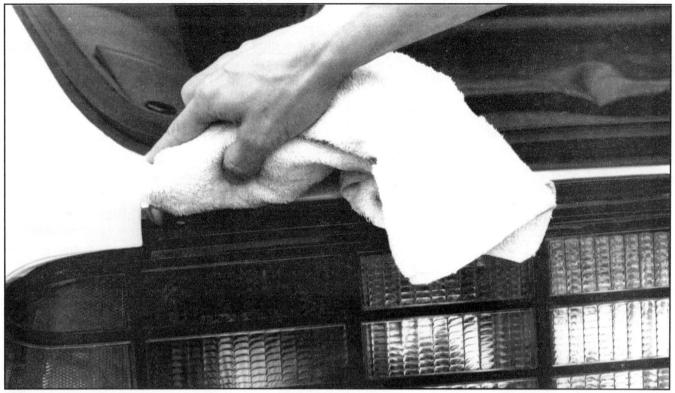

Remove all the excess wax from edges and indentations.

With a coat of wax, your car will regain a deep shine.

THE INTERIOR

"Dirt, dust and odor-free"

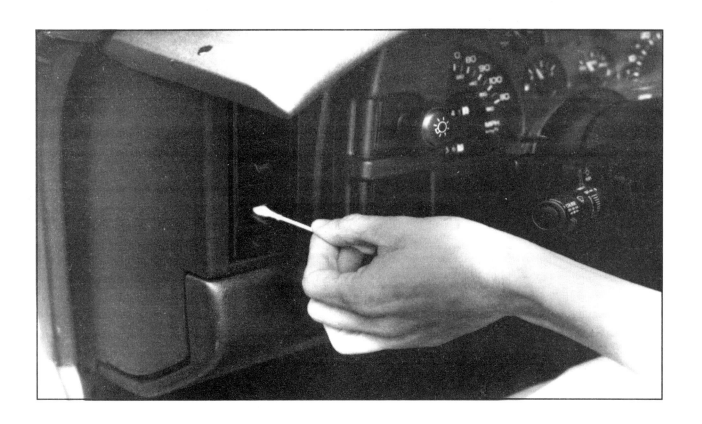

Now it's time to do a little housekeeping. It's time to clean the interior.

Like the engine compartment, this is an area a lot of people give only the slightest attention. After they have spent all their time cleaning the exterior of a cars, they shake out the floor mats, wipe off the dash and run a sweeper over the carpets. It's ironic that the one place where we spent the most of our time—the inside of the car—is the place where we spend the least time cleaning.

But cleaning the interior—including the trunk—should be considered a regular part of maintenance. Carpets will last longer if they are dirt-free, seats will hold up longer if they are kept clean, and the car will maintain its resale value much better with a regularly cleaned interior.

When you start on the interior, think of it as spring cleaning. Take everything out of the car that isn't bolted down—floormats, any loose carpets, accessories and, above all, trash. Slide the front seats all the way up and all the way back to make sure you have picked up everything. Empty the glove box and any map pockets on the doors or seats. Basically, remove everything you can.

Now clean the floor mats. If you have vinyl mats, this will simply be a matter of washing them with soap, water and a scrub brush. Allow them to dry completely before putting them back into the car.

If you have mats with carpet on them, first shake loose dirt out. Then, if it is at all possible, put them on a workbench or table of some sort and sweep them with a wisk broom. This will probably do more to remove dirt than anything else you could try. Professionals may use other, high-tech methods to extract dirt, but we have found this to be the best way.

Wash vinyl mats with soapy water.

Use a wisk broom to clean dirt out of carpeted mats.

A hand brush and the all-purpose
cleaner will get stains out of the carpet.

Next, spray the carpet on the mats with the all-purpose cleaner (such as Simple Green), putting only a light mist on them. There is no reason to soak the mats with the cleaner, since a light spraying will do a good job. You may want to spray a little bit more cleaner onto tough spots, but, even then, do not get the mats very wet.

Once you have sprayed the mats, scrub them with a hand brush. Try to brush the whole mat evenly and firmly, not concentrating just on the spots. When you finish, the mat should look like a piece of carpet that has just been vacuumed—with smooth, even swirls covering the entire mat. If you do run across stubborn stains, spray a little more cleaner on them and rub briskly with a toothbrush. Nearly all the dirt and stains in a carpet will be on the surface, so you should not have to try to clean too deeply. Because you have not soaked the mats, drying time should not be a problem, but if your carpets do seem damp, be sure to let them dry before putting them back in. This is one of the advantages of cleaning the carpets with an all-purpose cleaner rather than a shampoo: They are left so dry that there's no need to worry about wet floor mats.

If your car has other types of floormats—such as sisal or plastic, honeycombed mats—a simple shaking out is probably all that will be necessary. However, because these mats do not trap dirt, the carpets beneath them might require extra attention.

With the mats cleaned, it's time to start on the floor of the car itself. With a crevice tool on your vacuum, sweep out the entire car, being careful to clean out nooks and crannies where dirt can collect. Pay special attention to the areas between the seats and to the points where the seats are anchored to the floor of the car. Slide the seats all the way up and all the way back to make sure you get the whole floor clean. Sweep up any dirt or carpet lint that has collected around the bases of the seats, using a toothbrush to lift the dirt up to where the sweeper can suck it up. As you are cleaning the rest of the floor, keep the toothbrush handy in case you run across other places where dirt has collected in tight spots. Pay special attention to any places where the carpet meets vinyl or metal, using the toothbrush to free up the dirt and then the vacuum sweeper to remove it completely. Be sure to use the vacuum sweeper to clean any other carpeted parts of the car, such as on the doors. To get lint off of the carpets, roll a piece of masking tape around your hand so that the sticky side is on the outside and dab lightly over the surface of the carpet. This should remove most surface lint.

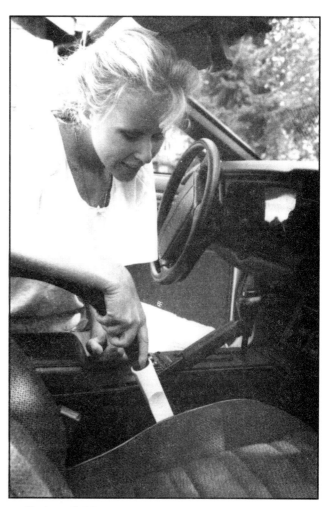

The long nozzle on the vacuum will clean tight areas.

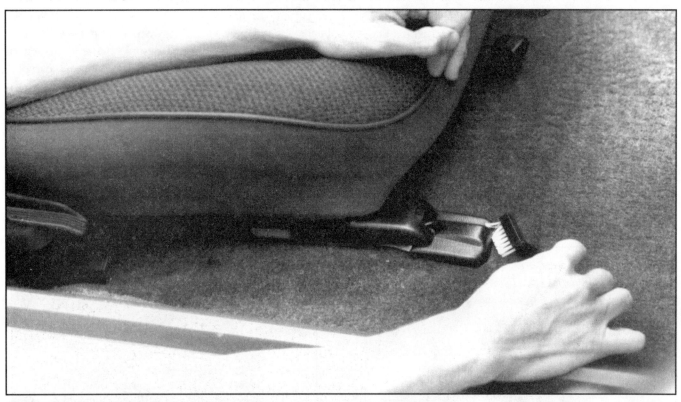

Use a toothbrush to clean dirt and lint off the tops of bolts and seat hardware.

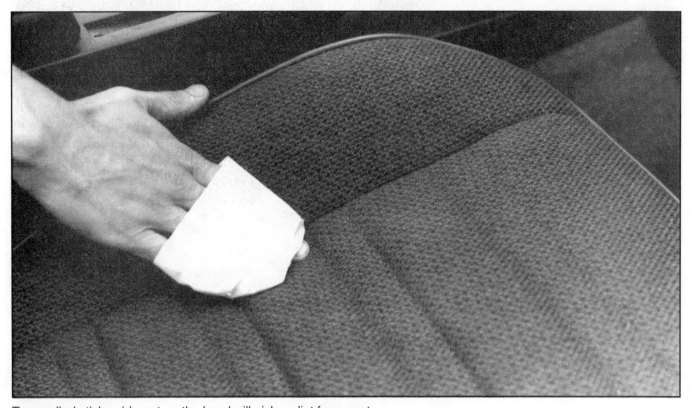

Tape rolled sticky-side-out on the hand will pick up lint from seats.

Next do the seats, using the nozzle of the sweeper to get deep down into the seats where dirt collects. Around the edges of the seats is a ridge of bolstering—use a toothbrush to loosen dirt out of those ridges all the way around the seats, again following-up with the vacuum sweeper. Move the seats in every way possible to make sure you get all the dirt.

Now you'll want to clean the carpets on the floor the same way you cleaned carpeted floor mats, with the all-purpose cleaner and a hand brush. Again, it is important that you use very little of the cleaner—a little goes a long way, so there is no reason to soak the carpets. The advantage here is the same as with the carpeted floormats: When you finish, you don't have to wait for your carpets to dry.

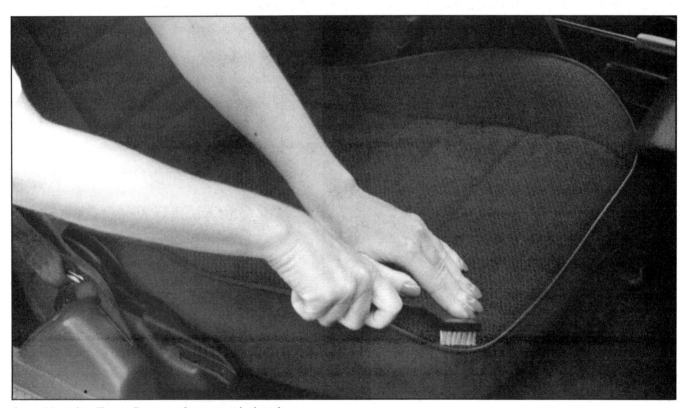

A toothbrush will get dirt away from seat bolstering.

Clean the carpets in the car in much the same way you did carpeted mats, with a brush and the all-purpose cleaner.

A spot remover will get out tough stains in carpets.

Spray an even mist of the cleaner onto the carpet, working a small area at a time. On tough spots, spray a little bit more, but remember that most of the dirt and stains will be on the surface of the carpet. Keep your toothbrush handy to get tight spots. Do the carpet on the doors and any other carpeted areas the same way. For really tough stains, a stronger cleaner may be used, but only in small amounts and with great care. For doing this, spray the cleaner onto your brush, not directly onto the stain. It is best to avoid using stronger chemicals unless it is absolutely necessary.

To clean your running boards, remove all screws, spray a little cleaner onto the boards and use a brush to get the dirt out of the grooves. Although you have already cleaned them when you did the door jambs, it's good to hit them again as part of the interior. Use the all-purpose cleaner and brush on arm rests and door handles as well, using the toothbrush to get dirt out of the areas where the door handles and arm rests meet the doors. Also scrub the tops of screws and bolts.

If you have scuff marks on the running boards or any other hard surface, spray some of the cleaner onto the brush and brush the spot away, using a towel to wipe off excess cleaner.

Clean the accelerator, brake and clutch pedals with the all-purpose cleaner, but DO NOT use a silicone-based product as a follow-up. This could make the pedals dangerously slick and could result in an accident. Simple cleaning is all that is needed with the pedals. Be sure they are completely dry before you drive.

A brush will loosen dirt in the running boards so the vacuum can pick it up.

The all-purpose cleaner and a brush will remove dirt from arm rests.

Clean the pedals with the all-purpose cleaner and a brush.

The cleaner you use on the interior may remove some of the painted lettering from hood-release levers, gear shift knobs and other surfaces, but these can be repainted using paint and a toothpick. On all of these surfaces, spray the cleaner onto a brush and brush the dirt away, following with a towel to wipe off excess cleaner.

To clean around the gear shift boot, first ENGAGE THE PARKING BRAKE and move the shift knob to different positions. Failing to engage the brake could result in a serious accident. Brush the cleaner on to the boot, making sure you get into every fold, and wipe it clean with a towel. Go through the rest of the interior, using the cleaner brush and towel to get dirt out of nooks and crannies. The brush will break up dirt that has collected in corners and the towel will clean it up.

To get into air vents, radio and heating and air conditioning controls, use the soft-bristle brush. This brush is stiff enough to get into tight spots and loosen up dirt yet gentle enough not to scratch the parts. Also use it around the steering wheel, turn signal controls and other dashboard controls, following the whole process with the vacuum cleaner to suck up the dirt the brush has broken free.

Repaint lettering on gear shift knobs using a toothpick.

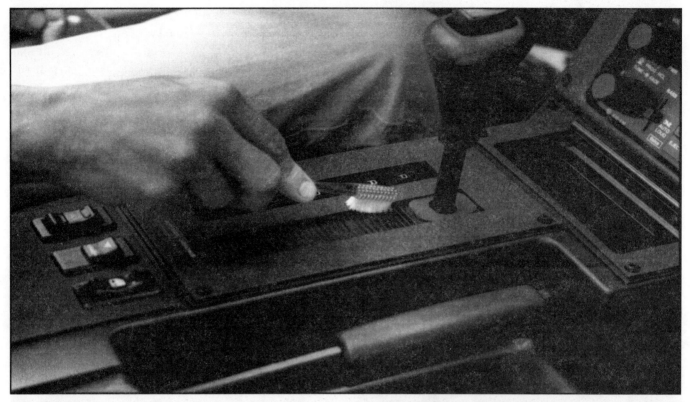

A toothbrush will get dirt out of tight places around the gear shift knob.

The soft bristle brush will clean without scratching the interior surfaces.

Open the glove box and use the soft-bristle brush to get dirt out of the corners, following up with the vacuum. A damp towel should pick up the dirt on the inside of the glove box. For any stubborn stains or scuff marks, use the all-purpose cleaner and a toothbrush.

Be sure to clean your ash trays, first dumping them out—be sure there are no hot ashes in them—then vacuuming them out. Use the solvent to break up any particularly tough spots. If an ashtray is in really bad shape, you may want to paint the inside of it with a high-heat paint. However, if you do decide to do this, pull the metal insert out of the ash tray and spray it separately. You should not need to paint the outside of the ashtray.

Flip down the visors, spraying a little cleaner onto the toothbrush and lightly cleaning the tops and bottoms of the visors. If the visors have mirrors on them, leave them down so you will

remember to clean the mirrors later when you do the rest of the glass.

It is probably not necessary to clean the headliner, but if there are any spots, remove them with a little of the all-purpose cleaner sprayed onto the tooth brush and follow-up with a towel.

At this time, you will also want to use the cleaner to remove spots from cloth or vinyl seats. Clean the edges of the seats and along the bolstering with the toothbrush and all-purpose cleaner. Again, remember that most stains are on the surface, so there is no need to soak the material—a light spray of the cleaner will do the job.

To clean leather seats, purchase a leather cleaner either form an automotive dealer or accessory shop or from a fine leather or luggage shop. Follow the directions on the product container.

Check the rest of the interior for marks or spots, applying the all-purpose cleaner sparingly with the toothbrush. While you do this, be careful not to spray

the cleaner into speakers since this could cause serious damage.

Now go over the interior again with the vacuum to pick up any dirt you may have broken free with the toothbrush and cleaner. To get dust and dirt off of the dash, a damp towel works as well as anything. While you are finishing with the final vacuuming, be sure to clean the area below the back window in cars without hatchbacks and to clean out the hatchback area in others. To get into the tight area below the back window, a wisk broom followed by the vacuum will work well.

If your car is not a hatchback, you'll want to clean the trunk now. Remove everything from the trunk and use the vacuum with the crevice tool to get all the dirt out of the nooks and crannies. Pull your spare tire out and clean under and around where it sits. You should also clean the tire, using soap and water. Leave it out until it dries.

Some people at this point might

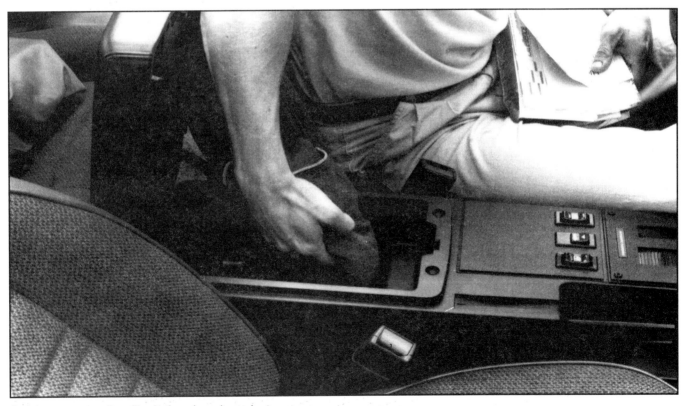

A damp rag usually will get the glove box clean.

Clean the visors with a toothbrush and the all-purpose cleaner.

Pull the spare tire and clean under and around where it sits.

want to apply a vinyl dressing to vinyl seats and to vinyl parts of the interior. We do not feel this is necessary, but, if you do choose to do this, follow label directions carefully, working the dressing *into* the vinyl and not just rubbing it onto the surface. Be sure to wipe away excess dressing so you don't end up with the residue that rubs off onto your clothes. If you choose not to use a vinyl dressing, we find that a thorough cleaning will give vinyl a clean look.

Leather dressing is important for leather seats. It, too, should be applied by rubbing it *into* the leather as opposed to simply wiping it on. Follow label directions, being sure, as with the vinyl dressing, to wipe away excess.

Next clean the windows, using a glass cleaner and paying special attention to the driver's side of the windshield. If you have a T-top, take it out and clean both sides of the glass and, using the all-purpose cleaner and a toothbrush, clean the area where the T-top fits into the roof.

A thorough cleaning should remove any odors inside your car, but if there is a persistent odor you may want to spray a household air freshener into the car, being sure to spray some onto the underside of the seats. While car fresheners can be bought and some car washes offer air freshener machines, we have found that household air fresheners give the best results.

Clean all glass with a glass cleaner and a towel.

Leather seats should be treated with a leather dressing.

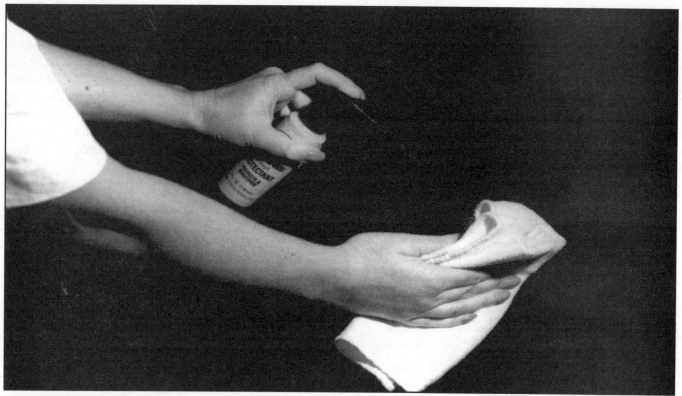

Vinyl seats may be treated with a vinyl dressing.

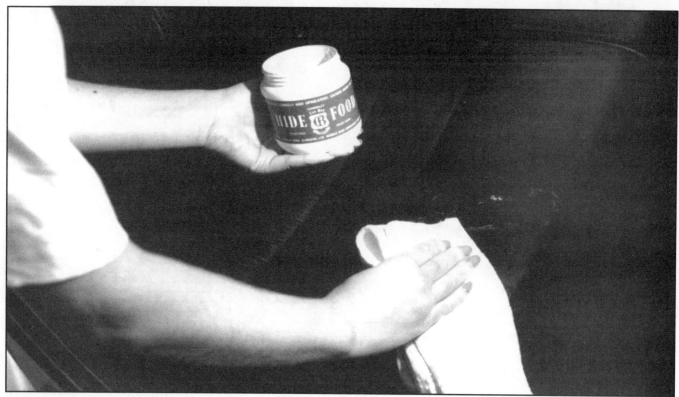

Leather seats should be treated with a leather dressing.

Clean all glass with a glass cleaner and a towel.

Remove t-tops and clean around where they sit on the car.

An air freshener sprayed under the seats should kill persistent odors.

A clean interior adds to the overall appearance of a car.

CHAPTER FOUR

FINISHING TOUCHES

"Shine, sparkle and gloss"

Since you have completed the cleaning of your interior, your work is nearly done. All that remains are the finishing touches—some of the "details" that give detailing its name.

Throughout this book, we have given you steps that make the difference between simply cleaning your car and detailing it, from cleaning the engine to brushing the dust out of the nooks and crannies in your dash. Now, with 14 simple steps, we're going to show you how to take your car up even one more notch:

1. Clean non-chrome exhaust tips with fine-grade steel wool, removing old rust and dirt, and then paint them with high-heat paint. In doing so, be sure to mask off all surrounding areas and apply the paint carefully and sparingly. Chrome exhaust tips should be cleaned with the all-purpose cleaner and fine-grade steel wool, if necessary.

Exhaust tips can be painted with high-heat paint.

Steel wool will clean chrome exhaust tips.

2. Remove excess wax or compound from hood, trunk and door edges and from decorations—particularly insignia—by brushing it away with a soft-bristled detail brush, and then following up with a towel.

Remove excess wax with a soft-bristle detail brush.

3. Clean the outside of the windows with a fine (grade #0000) steel wool to remove water spots or anything else you might have missed. CAUTION: Do not clean mirrors or soft-top rear windows with steel wool—they are softer and will be seriously damaged by this process.

Fine-grade steel wool will remove water spots from windows.

4. Paint wheel wells with a flat black paint to improve the car's overall appearance. This is purely cosmetic and will wear away over time, but some people really like the appearance this gives the car. However, do not paint plastic wheel wells, and use the paint sparingly.

Painted wheel wells make tires and wheels stand out.

5. Clean all (uncoated) chrome trim with the fine steel wool. CAUTION: Some trim has a plastic coating on it. Using steel wool will damage this coating.

6. Dress any vinyl on the car if you wish, applying dressing lightly to all vinyl surfaces and removing excess with a towel.

7. Touch up paint chips. If you decide to do this—repairing rock chips on the front of the car and other problems in the paint—be sure to use the correct color of paint. Most cars will have necessary information for getting the correct color printed on the identification plate under the hood. Different types of cars have different ways of identifying the paint color, so consult your dealer. You will only want to apply a small amount of paint to each chip, and a toothpick is usually the best tool for applying the paint.

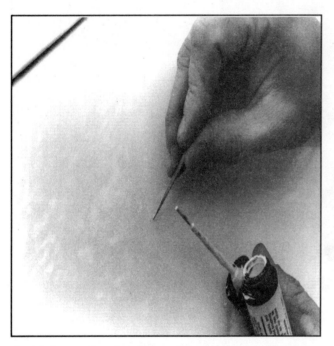

Carefully repair paint chips using the correct color of paint and a toothpick.

8. Dress the tires with silicone. Be sure that when you do this the wind is not blowing or you will get the spray silicone on your freshly detailed car.

Dress the tires with a silicone-based product.

9. Check the wheels one last time to make sure you haven't missed any spots and to wipe off excess tire dressing that may have found its way onto wheels.

Wipe away any tire dressing that may have found its way onto the wheels.

10. Wipe the silicone off of the engine parts (applied in Chapter Two), using a towel that is used for no other purpose.

11. Apply a rubber treatment to the rubber or synthetic weather stripping around doors, windows the trunk, hood or any other areas. The rubber treatment will not only improve the look of the car, it will also prolong the life and effectiveness of the seals.

12. If you wish, you may apply a mag/wheel polish. Although regular cleaning and maintenance will keep most wheels looking good, some car owners prefer to use wheel polish. Follow label directions closely.

A rubber treatment on weather stripping will help preserve it.

13. Go through your interior one last time, using cotton swabs and toothpicks to clear dust out of vents and other nooks and crannies on the dash board.

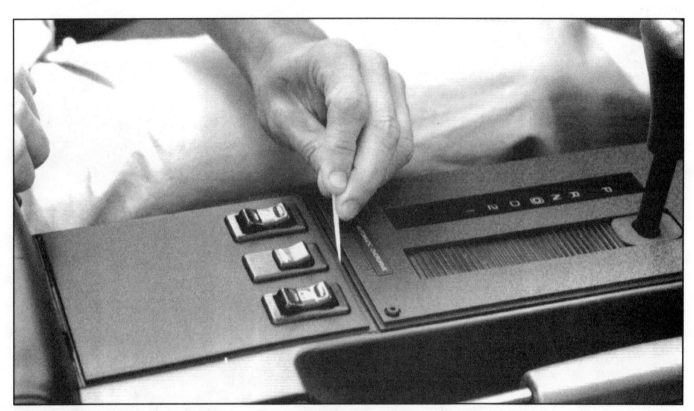

Make one last pass through the interior with cotton swabs and toothpicks.

14. Walk around the car with a toothpick, cotton swab and a clean towel, checking any spots on the car where wax may have been missed. Pay special attention to the areas around and within insignia and all edges (such as around the hood, trunk and doors). Clean the wax away with the toothpick or swab, following up with the towel to make sure it has all been removed.

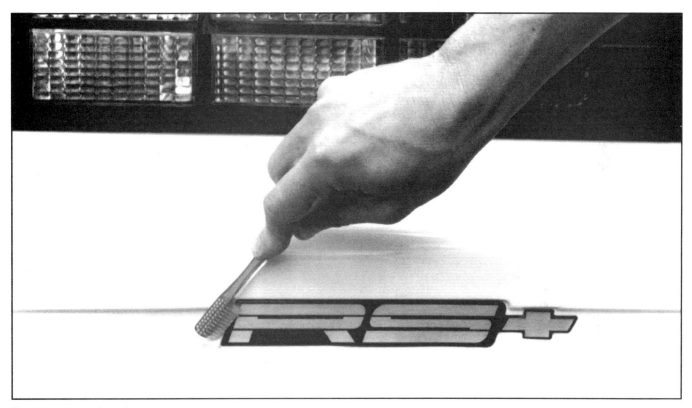

Remove any missed excess wax.

Now stand back and admire your work, checking to make sure you haven't missed any spots. No matter how careful you may have been, it always helps to give the car one last inspection—besides, you'll enjoy looking over your newly detailed car.

Step back and admire your work.